L 8/15

Need to Know
LSD

Sean Connolly

www.heinemann.co.uk
visit our website to find out more information about **Heinemann Library** books.

To order:
☎ Phone 44 (0) 1865 888066
📄 Send a fax to 44 (0) 1865 314091
💻 Visit the Heinemann Bookshop at www.heinemann.co.uk to browse our catalogue and order online.

First published in Great Britain by Heinemann Library, Halley Court, Jordan Hill, Oxford OX2 8EJ,
a division of Reed Educational and Professional Publishing Ltd.

Heinemann is a registered trademark of Reed Educational & Professional Publishing Limited.

Oxford Melbourne Auckland Johannesburg Blantyre Gaborone Ibadan Portsmouth NH (USA) Chicago

Designed by M2 Graphic Design
Printed in Hong Kong / China
Originated by Ambassador Litho Ltd.

04 03 02 01 00
10 9 8 7 6 5 4 3 2 1

ISBN 0431 097763

British Library Cataloguing in Publication Data
Sean Connolly
LSD – (Need to know)
1. LSD (Drug) – Juvenile literature 2. LSD (Drug) – Physiological effect – Juvenile literature
I. Title 362.2'94

Acknowledgements
The Publishers would like to thank the following for permission to reproduce photographs: Associated Press:
pg.21; Bubbles: Pauline Cutter pg.32, Loisjoy Thurston pg.35, Pauline Cutter pg.39, Jennie Woodcock
pg.44, Dr Hercules Robinson pg.49; David Hoffman: pg.8; Holt Studios: Nigel Cattlin pg.6, pg.7; Hulton
Getty: pg.11, pg.15, pg.18; Impact: Eliza Armstrong pg.5, Mohamed Ansar pg.22, Peter Arkell pg.29; PA
News: pg.25, pg.40; Photofusion: Liam Bailey pg.27; Retna: Jenny Acheson pg.51; Rex Features: pg.12,
pg.17, pg.31, pg.37; Ronald Grant Archive: pg.9, pg.19; Science Photo Library: pg.34, pg.42, pg.47.

Cover photograph reproduced with permission of Science Photo Library.

Every effort has been made to contact copyright holders of any material reproduced in this book.
Any omissions will be rectified in subsequent printings if notice is given to the publisher.

Any words appearing in the text in bold, **like this**, are explained in the Glossary.

Contents

Introduction

LSD is the most common **hallucinogen** as well as being one of the most **potent** drugs known to science. It only takes a microscopic amount of the drug to produce a powerful experience, or 'trip', which lasts up to twelve hours. During this trip, the LSD user encounters a bewildering array of images and sounds, sometimes jumbled together or exaggerated into strange distortions. The 'real world' seems to recede into the dim memory and is replaced with the new sensations which rush through the mind. Added to this heady brew, no two trips are identical but some of their effects can recur long after the trip is over, in the form of **flashbacks**.

Myth and reality

Considering the power of LSD, it is not surprising that a number of claims and counter-claims have been made about it. Ardent supporters believe it unlocks reserves of mental powers that can help worldwide understanding. Opponents of the drug have claimed, over the years, that it can damage **chromosomes**, drive people crazy or trigger mental illnesses such as **schizophrenia**.

The truth obviously lies somewhere between the extremes of these opposing camps, although it would be foolish to rule out all aspects of the long term consequences on mental health of using LSD. What is agreed is that we are still not aware of all there is to know about this powerful drug, or indeed quite how it exerts such an effect on the brain.

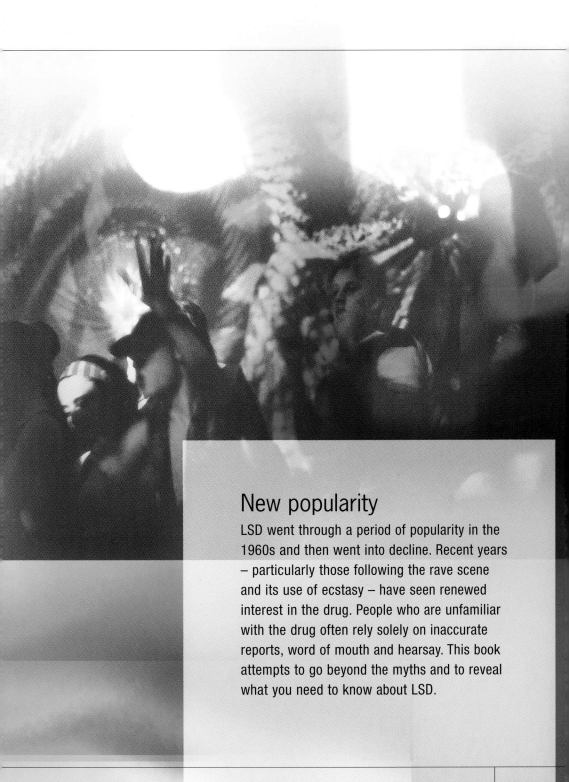

New popularity

LSD went through a period of popularity in the 1960s and then went into decline. Recent years – particularly those following the rave scene and its use of ecstasy – have seen renewed interest in the drug. People who are unfamiliar with the drug often rely solely on inaccurate reports, word of mouth and hearsay. This book attempts to go beyond the myths and to reveal what you need to know about LSD.

What is LSD?

LSD is a **synthetic** substance manufactured from ergot, a **parasitic** fungus which grows naturally on rye and other grasses. The initials LSD stand for the chemical name of the substance – lysergic acid diethylamide. Another common name for the drug is 'acid', again referring to its chemical make-up. LSD is very powerful and only a tiny amount has a **hallucinogenic** effect.

A trip

LSD has a powerful effect on the mind. After taking the drug, which is odourless and colourless but with a slightly bitter taste, the user begins to experience the hallucinogenic effects known as a 'trip'. The first effects begin about half an hour after taking the LSD; the effects reach a peak about six hours later and then fade after about twelve hours. Unlike many other drugs, LSD produces very few physical changes – the pupils of the eyes **dilate** somewhat and the body temperature rises slightly.

The actual experience of a trip is mental. It differs from individual to individual and even from time to time. Much depends on the mood of the person taking the drug, and on the setting – whether they take it when they are alone or with a group of trusted friends. Most users experience distorted shapes, intense colours and even movement in stationary objects. There are also changes to hearing and in the sense of time and place. These changes in perception are usually described as **hallucinations**, although for the most part an LSD user will know that the changes are not real.

Helpless feelings

Although someone on an LSD trip is usually able to distinguish reality from drug-induced changes, these distortions can be upsetting and disturbing. Because there is no way of stopping a trip once it has started, the result can be a frightening experience called a 'bad trip'. People who have this experience often report feelings of dizziness, anxiety, disorientation and even **paranoia**.

The naturally occuring fungus ergot forms the basis for LSD, one of the most powerful of all mind-altering drugs. It grows on rye and other grasses.

What is LSD?

Different trips

LSD is one of many drugs that people take for their **hallucinogenic** effects. Some of these drugs are found naturally in plants that people collect. The closest effects to those of LSD come from 'magic mushrooms', in which the active **compounds** psilocybin and psilocin react with the body's nervous system. The peyote cactus of North America contains mescaline, which also acts as a powerful **hallucinogen**. The trips from these plant-based drugs tend to be slightly shorter than an LSD trip, lasting about four hours.

Other hallucinogens are produced chemically. Some people take phencyclidine (PCP), also known as 'Angel dust', in order to achieve an experience like that of an LSD trip, although the sensation often leads to anxiety and panic. MDMA, better known as ecstasy, produces a high that people describe as a mild version of that of LSD – it doesn't induce **hallucinations** but it does make sounds and colours seem more intense.

Much of the LSD sold today comes in blotting paper strips with a logo on each 'dose'.

Millions of doses

Chemically produced LSD is a white, odourless material that appears in crystal form. In this form it is purchased in amounts weighing up to about 10 grams. Then the LSD is diluted into thousands or even millions of individual doses. Darker-coloured LSD is usually the result of an imperfection in the manufacturing process, so producers often apply the drug to tan or yellow-coloured paper to disguise the discolouration.

At the 'retail' level, LSD is usually sold by word of mouth. People exchange addresses and telephone numbers to ensure a steady supply. This unofficial network also links users with unofficial organizations that champion the use of LSD and the lifestyle that goes with it. An increasing number of Internet websites act as message exchanges for both distributors and users worldwide.

Widespread fear about LSD in the 1960s led to a series of lurid films.

The 'big bang'

The **pharmaceutical** industry in the early decades of the twentieth century worked busily, trying to isolate new drugs that could be used for medical purposes. One such company, Sandoz, based in the Swiss city of Basel, had devoted much of its research into *Claviceps purpurea*, better known as ergot, a type of fungus that grows on diseased kernels of rye. Ergot had been known as a folk medicine as long ago as the Middle Ages, when it was used as an aid in childbirth.

The first 'trip'

The Sandoz scientist in charge of the ergot project, Albert Hoffmann, began **synthesizing** the building blocks – or **molecules** – of ergot in the mid-1930s. He worked carefully, noting each new **compound** and testing it on animals. His aim was to find a drug that would cure painful conditions such as **migraine**. By 1943 he had reached the twenty-fifth compound that had Lysergic Acid Diethylamide (LSD) as its base. The previous twenty-four had had no effect on animals so Hoffmann took a tiny amount of LSD-25 himself. The result was astounding. Within half an hour he was dizzy and beginning to laugh uncontrollably. As he rode his bicycle home, the road and pavement seemed to swirl and twist and the colours around him had become extremely vivid. Sounds also became distorted. In short, Hoffmann was undergoing the first LSD 'trip'.

"At home I sank into a not unpleasant intoxicated-like condition, characterized by an extremely stimulated imagination. In a dreamlike state, with eyes closed, I perceived an uninterrupted stream of fantastic pictures, extraordinary shapes with intense kaleidoscopic play of colours. After some two hours the condition faded away."

(Albert Hoffmann describing his LSD experience in *LSD: My Problem Child*)

Swiss chemist Albert Hoffman was one of the first people to recognize the significance of LSD.

The 'big bang'

Unknown powers

Hoffmann had accidentally discovered one of the most powerful drugs ever developed. The following morning, however, he felt normal again – apart from a heightened appreciation of colours and sounds that reminded him of his experience the previous night. Indeed, Hoffmann was able to recall nearly everything that had occurred during the 'trip' and he concluded that he must have retained **consciousness** throughout.

As a properly trained scientist, Hoffmann knew that his experience might have been a one-off, so he wrote a report for the Sandoz research department that dealt with new discoveries. They decided to test the drug in various doses on a wide range of animals. In each case, there were strange developments. Spiders on a low dose of LSD wove incredibly complex webs – but with higher doses did no weaving at all. Cats grew very excited. A chimp was given LSD and put among other chimps. The result was chaos – the LSD chimp ignored all the usual 'rules' that govern life in a chimp colony and the other animals were completely confused. The Sandoz team knew that they had found a powerful drug but they had no real idea of how it worked or what its overall effects on humans might be.

Tool for psychology

The time had come for more tests – this time on humans. Volunteers, including a psychiatrist with links to Sandoz, began to file a series of reports about their own experiences. One common reaction seemed to emerge. In low doses, LSD seemed able to unleash memories that had long been **suppressed**. This news suggested that LSD might become a valuable aid in psychotherapy, a field of science that also aimed to help patients by allowing them to deal with their own memories. Among the conditions that LSD was said to cure were **schizophrenia**, criminal behaviour and **alcoholism**. It was at this stage that Sandoz began recommending that psychologists take LSD themselves 'to gain an understanding of the **subjective** experiences of the schizophrenic'. Following this advice many psychology students took the drug at university.

Throughout the 1950s psychologists used LSD to relax patients and to free their memories. They also took the drug to help them understand how the patients themselves felt. Psychologists in the UK and the United States used LSD to treat alcohol and drug addiction. The drug was also used on terminally ill patients to ease pain and help them face death. But most of all, psychologists valued the way LSD could deliver a 'big bang' to the memory and release a series of buried memories. The US military saw this as a chance to create a drug that could disable an army without using any weapons.

Film star Cary Grant was one of the high-profile people who took LSD as part of psychological therapy in the 1950s.

The LSD industry

When Sandoz Laboratories began developing LSD in the 1940s they soon realized that they had developed the most powerful **hallucinogenic** substance known to man. Albert Hoffmann's initial caution about the dosages was well placed. Dosages of LSD are measured in micrograms, or millionths of a gram. By comparison, dosages of heroin and cocaine are measured in milligrams, or thousandths of a gram. LSD is reckoned to be 100 times more **potent** than the hallucinogenic drug psilocybin and 4000 times stronger than mescaline – and both of these drugs were treated with caution before LSD arrived on the scene.

Looking for benefits

At first Sandoz tried and failed to find some form of medical use for the new drug – it did not work as a **stimulant** to the **respiratory** or circulatory systems. The experiences of Hoffmann and several other human 'guinea pigs', however, sent researchers looking into an area where LSD would remain lodged for nearly six decades – the human mind.

By 1947 Sandoz had begun producing LSD in large enough amounts to be sold commercially. They gave the drug the name 'Delysid' and **marketed** it as a psychological cure-all.

Henry Luce Robinson was the co-founder of the American weekly news magazine *Time.* A fervent anti-Communist, he is known to have taken LSD at a time when some scientists believed LSD was a mind-enhancing drug.

The LSD industry

Powerful suppliers

Other companies, such as Eli Lilly in the United States and Spofa in Czechoslovakia, also began producing large quantities of LSD in the late 1940s. They also emphasized the powerful **psychological** effects of the new drug. Soon LSD gained the reputation as the drug linked with the highly educated. After all, it had been developed by a trained research chemist and popularized by high-ranking members of the psychological community. Unlike other drugs, such as cannabis, which start out being popular with ordinary people and then 'work upwards', LSD began as a creation of the highly trained and 'worked outwards'. More and more people learned of its existence, largely because those who used it were able to spread the word through lectures and educational articles.

Among those who became interested in LSD were the military and **intelligence** communities. They saw the drug as a psychological tool and weapon. Starting in the 1950s, the US intelligence agency, the CIA, began twenty years of tests on LSD.

They saw it both as a way of **demoralizing** an enemy and of reversing the effects of **brainwashing**. Tests were carried out both on prisoners taken during the Korean War and on American soldiers. Behind these tests was the hope that the 'big bang', which psychologists had promised, would transform itself into a powerful weapon.

The wider arena

Although the military carried out many of these experiments themselves, using their own supplies of LSD, they turned to leading universities for more detailed studies. By this time, in the late 1950s, the academic studies took on a different tone and the flow of LSD increased. A former American spy, 'Captain' Al Hubbard, bought a vast amount of LSD from Sandoz and distributed it among his friends in the worlds of art, industry, science and even the clergy. Two psychologists at Harvard University, Timothy Leary and Richard Alpert, were well placed to observe and document the new trends.

Many of the military tests were carried out at Harvard and, in addition, the two men moved in the circles where people had been offered some of Hubbard's supplies. They quickly turned their attention to the field of '**psychedelic** research' and they made many new friends who would help them spread the popularity of LSD. One of the most famous was the British author Aldous Huxley, who had long been a champion of research into the inner mysteries of the human mind.

The shifting lights of psychedelic rock shows, with music by bands such as the Grateful Dead (above), echoed the experience of an LSD trip.

"You must expect opposition. There are people in this society who will do everything within their considerable power to stop our research."

(Aldous Huxley to Timothy Leary, 1960, quoted in *Street Drugs*, by Andrew Tyler)

Power to the people?

Timothy Leary's involvement with LSD (see panel) was a fitting start to the 1960s, a decade which – more than any other – has become associated with LSD. The LSD 'industry' as we now know it – illegal and **underground**, as opposed to legal and linked to science – also developed during that time. With Leary and Alpert as champions of the new cause, word spread very quickly. Many young people were influenced by the promises of expanded **consciousness** and inner fulfilment. The promises – and the tests that backed them up – were seen as a threat by those in authority. The pair lost their Harvard teaching positions in 1963, roughly at the same time as another charismatic figure arrived on the scene to publicize LSD and its effects.

Author Ken Kesey (left) encouraged many people to take LSD. His book *One Flew over the Cuckoo's Nest* (a scene from the film version with Jack Nicholson is shown right) was inspired by his own experiences as an LSD 'guinea pig'.

'Mad chemists'

If Leary and Alpert represented a continuation of the 'old-fashioned', scientific approach to LSD – however unconventional their methods appeared – their 'rival' on the West coast of the United States was in many ways the face of the LSD future. Ken Kesey was a young author who had written two highly praised novels, including the famous *One Flew over the Cuckoo's Nest*. Like Alpert and Leary, he had taken LSD and believed that the public should share the secret.

However; with Kesey there was one big difference – he did not operate within the realms of academic science. Therefore, he had no need to treat his LSD experiments as anything other than recreation or pleasure. Throughout 1964 and 1965, when LSD was still legal and in plentiful supply, Kesey assembled a group of young people who were eager to test the new drug in nearly every circumstance possible. The group was known as the 'Merry Pranksters' and lived up to its name by attracting hundreds of people to LSD parties across California. At some of these parties – very much like today's raves – they had large bowls of 'punch' spiked with LSD.

Power to the people?

The crackdown

Following the efforts of Kesey and similar figures in Britain and other countries, use of LSD increased dramatically in the mid-1960s. Along with this came disturbing reports of the drug's power. By 1966 the public outcry became very loud and the United States and the UK – quickly followed by most other countries – outlawed the drug.

By 1968 LSD had stopped being prescribed for the few remaining **psychological** conditions it was meant to treat. From that time onwards, the whole LSD industry went **underground**. A select group of chemists, however, had studied the complex formulae needed to produce the drug. This group, known as 'cooks', were able to produce large amounts of LSD which could supply all of the United States; similar 'cooks' were at work in Europe. The cooks guarded their 'recipes' closely, occasionally passing the formula down to others but on the whole limiting production to a very small band of individuals.

This system has continued for more than thirty years. Even now, drug-control authorities estimate that fewer than a dozen 'cooks' produce all of the LSD that is distributed in the United States. Similar LSD-producing **elites** exist in other countries.

The LSD 'guru'

The name of Timothy Leary crops up again and again when the history and significance of LSD are discussed. Leary, born in 1920 in Massachusetts, was no doubt the first person to build a wide public stage for the drug. It was Leary's experiments, conducted in scientific surroundings in the early 1960s, that seemed to promise miracles from the powerful drug. In 1966 he formed a **psychedelic** religion, the League for Spiritual Discovery, and got people to invest money in his research centre in Millbrook, New York. However, with LSD being made illegal, he found himself arrested some ten times before seeking **asylum** in Switzerland. Leary was sent back to the United States in 1973 and spent three years in prison. After his release in 1976 he turned away from drugs and began to speak about the power of the communication revolution. Throughout the 1980s he wrote books and computer software; his lectures now focused on computer technology and the Internet. Leary was diagnosed as having prostate cancer in the early 1990s and died in 1996.

"If you can remember the sixties, you weren't there."

(Popular saying, referring to the widespread use of LSD and other drugs)

Who takes LSD?

Many people believe that fashion moves in cycles. Clothing, furniture and music that are scorned in one decade reappear as high fashion or 'cool' statements only a few years later. In the 1990s it once more became acceptable to appreciate things from the 1960s. Feature films such as *Austin Powers* and *Lost in Space* celebrated sixties culture; groups such as Oasis and Kula Shaker recalled the Beatles and even the word 'cool' itself achieved more of its 1960s popularity.

The trip continues

Even if some of these trends have made gentle fun of the past, there have been several important similarities between the decades. One major link has been the great interest in the 'counterculture'. Whereas people in the 1960s were rebelling against the stifling 1950s, many people in the 1990s were turning their backs on what they saw as the selfishness of the 1980s. This attitude is reflected in the popularity in books about the New Age and spirituality in general.

Spiritual pursuits such as meditation, like the renewed poularity of LSD, are links to the enduring legacy of the 1960s.

All of these trends meant that the time was ripe for the return of a drug that seems to promise increased self-awareness and gentleness. Many LSD users today are as convinced as were those of thirty years ago that the drug opens a gateway to greater understanding and brotherhood.

The party scene

The other big spur to taking LSD nowadays is the rave culture, or dance scene. Many young people have grown accustomed to taking ecstasy and dancing all night. LSD – both cheaper and more powerful than ecstasy – has the power to provide the necessary prolonged high. Those who take LSD in these circumstances do not aim to change the world. They only want to dance the night away – high on a drug that takes the pulsating music into another dimension.

Widening appeal

One big difference between today's LSD picture and that of the 1960s is the age group involved. When LSD first became relatively widespread it was mainly people in their late teens and early twenties who took it. Surveys in the 1990s, however, show that many younger people are experimenting with the drug. UK surveys suggest that 10–15 per cent of 15- and 16-year-olds have tried LSD.

The big attraction

The mental 'kick' provided by LSD is a powerful attraction for some people. They enjoy the distortions that accompany 'hearing' colours and 'seeing' sounds or the movement of patterns on wallpaper or paintings. The term 'trip' arose when some of the first LSD users compared their experience to a trip inside the mind. Although it is hard to describe what anyone will meet in the course of this trip, regular users sense a feeling of heightened self-awareness. They may also feel that their trip has a **mystical** or spiritual element.

Open to suggestion

A person who experiences feelings of grandeur and unusually high sensitivity while taking LSD probably started the trip expecting some sort of **enlightenment** or 'breakthrough'. Likewise, someone undergoing a 'bad trip' probably started out feeling generally anxious or worried about the effects of the drug. These experiences point to a basic **contradiction** about LSD: although the effects of a single trip are unpredictable, the overall experience depends much more than other drugs on surroundings and suggestion.

Experienced LSD users claim to be able to steer a trip towards an area they wish to explore. They also say that a frightened first-time user can be similarly steered away from the worst effects of a bad trip.

British police seized this load of LSD in 1978. It contained enough LSD for 670,000 doses and had a street value of £1 million – a figure that would be much higher now.

Taking LSD

The tiny amounts of LSD needed for a trip are astounding – only 300 millionths of a gram are enough to produce a trip that distorts the mind for twelve hours. This small dose of LSD is usually mixed with alcohol and then small bits of paper are soaked in the solution. This preparation is called 'blotter acid', after the blotting paper that is used. The paper is often 'trade-marked' with various designs such as 'star wave', 'white dove' and 'strawberry'. LSD is less commonly available in gelatine sheets, sugar cubes or formed into tablets or capsules.

Where LSD is found

Despite sending each user on a hair-raising trip into their own mind – and producing half a day's worth of altered perception – LSD tends to be associated with groups. In the 1960s, when LSD first hit the headlines, it was the hippies who were linked with the drug. At concerts and festivals or simply 'crashing out' in someone's house, they usually took LSD together.

Much of the hippy mentality of peace and love arose from the sense of helping each other avoid an unsettling experience. For them, life was about peace and harmony and, above all, sharing: the idea of taking LSD for oneself was seen as selfish. Modern users share many of these views, even if the whole hippy scene has become social history.

Certain risks

Although many LSD users scoff at the stories of suicides or instant insanity traced to a single use of 'acid', there are many areas in which an LSD experience would be very dangerous. People who have taken a small amount of alcohol, cocaine or amphetamines believe that they can still concentrate on most tasks. LSD is different: it dominates the brain while the trip is in progress, making it almost impossible to perform anything that requires concentration. Driving a car or operating any sort of machinery becomes a recipe for disaster for someone on an LSD trip.

Still rolling

Ken Kesey, a widely respected American author, had been an LSD test volunteer in the early 1960s and had also concluded that the public could learn by taking the drug. Unlike members of the scientific community, however, Kesey's approach was carefree. He had a group of young followers who called themselves the Merry Pranksters. In 1964 they toured America in a brightly painted bus, playing musical instruments and making hours of film. They organized concerts in California where tubs of soft drinks were laced with LSD. Kesey was later arrested and spent time in prison. In the 1990s, however, he and a new generation of Pranksters were still spreading the message of cutting loose from society – even if this time they weren't recommending LSD as the vehicle for that trip.

The LSD lifestyle

Someone who drinks a lot of alcohol can still manage to work, even while recognizing a problem with alcohol **dependence**. The same is true for users of amphetamines, cannabis and cocaine. In each case, the 'high' wears off after a few hours, leaving the user free to do other things afterwards.

The time commitment

A regular LSD user is different. Apart from taking the drug only on weekends – which themselves would be wiped out by just one LSD dose – there is no way to mix LSD with a normal routine. The trip becomes not just the most important element in the user's day – it is the only element. It goes without saying that someone who has just taken LSD will be virtually rooted to the spot for the next twelve hours, since driving is out of the question and daily activities such as catching a bus assume nightmarish proportions.

Typically, a casual weekend user will take the drug in the late afternoon or early evening, depending on the setting. It is usually earlier if the person is staying inside with friends, or later in a more public setting such as a festival or rave. After about half an hour, the trip takes over and the LSD user has no choice but to ride it out.

The setting

Most people take LSD in a group, preferably among people they know and feel they can trust. There are few feelings more upsetting than experiencing a bad trip, and regular users try to lessen the effects of a bad trip by counting on the support of the friends around them. These familiar, or at least pleasant, surroundings make up what most LSD users refer to as the 'setting'.

The small group who have taken LSD go quiet for about the first half hour, then giggles and muted laughter take over. The drug has begun to take effect. It is no exaggeration to describe the next twelve hours as a mental roller-coaster ride, with mood changes often accompanying the dazzling array of images flashing before the eyes – whether they are open or closed. Typically, the trip leaves the user with a profound sense of tiredness and generally feeling drained.

Regular use of LSD could cause someone to 'drop out' of the school scene at a time when young people should be maturing and building friendships.

The LSD lifestyle

A kids' drug?

Despite its ability to provide a powerful high for up to twelve hours, LSD is often referred to as a 'kids' drug'. This seems puzzling at first, but on closer examination there are several reasons why it may be true. The time commitment is one obvious reason – no one working hard at school or with a steady job could possibly combine the LSD experience with a disciplined routine. The second reason relates to the 'kick' itself. If a mature adult knows that it is best, for example, to drink in **moderation**, then the crazy sequence of events in an LSD trip must represent the exact opposite. The need to blot out the real world and escape into yourself reveals a powerful sense of selfishness.

LSD has been used **recreationally** for more than three decades, and yet there are many similarities about the people who have taken it over the years. Extensive studies in the United States indicate that the average LSD user is male and in his late teens or early twenties. Although the percentage of young men who have taken LSD has risen within this group, the trend does not seem to have spread beyond.

Getting hold of LSD

Because it is so concentrated, LSD can be produced in huge quantities at very little cost. Once someone has learned of it, usually through word of mouth, LSD is easy to buy. It is compact and easy to conceal. These factors, plus the low cost of actually buying the drug, mean that LSD can easily gain a foothold in the community.

Not so safe

Many LSD users point out that the original 'scare' stories about the drug were not based on truth. They can also show that other drugs such as cocaine cause as many as forty times more hospital emergencies than LSD does. Nevertheless, the LSD figure is concentrated more in a younger age group: in 1993 LSD ranked fourth as a cause of US medical emergencies, after alcohol/drug combinations, marijuana and cocaine.

Family and friends

As a rule, people who use LSD regularly do not display any physical signs of the activity – unlike prolonged users of amphetamines, alcohol or heroin. At home they might be inclined to lie in a bit longer, but the rest of the family would probably assume that this was caused by very late nights. Real changes in their life would only become obvious if they were to start taking the drug during the week. Then the missed school, fatigue and strange lack of normal **motivation** would really stand out.

Effects on friendships

Usually, friends have a better idea of what is going on among their own group. Apart from simply learning through the grapevine that someone was 'dropping acid', they would soon recognize the changes. Taking LSD is – and always has been – seen as crossing a threshold. The **psychological** and behavioural effects of taking LSD for the first time represent much more of a milestone than taking the first drink of alcohol.

Even if there is less of a **stigma** attached to taking LSD among young people than there is among their parents, they still recognize that it is an intensely powerful drug. Many people feel concerned about being drawn in, through **peer pressure**, to a threatening world of mind games. At the same time, users often feel that those 'left behind' are stuck in a dull life, and as a result they might break off the friendship. Add to this the fact that a non-user has no real means of connecting with someone who is tripping on LSD. This huge gap – dominating all of the user's leisure time – pushes many friendships beyond breaking point.

New directions

A small handful of dried 'magic mushrooms' (left) can produce an experience like that of an LSD trip.

After its period of decline in the 1970s and then its return to popularity in the 1990s, LSD has become both plentiful and cheap. In real terms – taking into account **inflation** – the drug is probably cheaper than it ever was. Most people pay about £2-5 for a 'tab', the typical single dose. One big difference between today's **market** for LSD and that in the 1960s is that the whole process seems more commercial.

The 1990s might be described as a 'caring, sharing' decade but the hard-nosed business values of the 1980s are evident in the way LSD is sold.

Mysterious, blank sheets of blotting paper have been replaced with tabs that appear to have been produced by a major company. Even the emblems that appear on the tabs have a more sophisticated look – using **topical** images such as Bart Simpson or Saddam Hussein as **logos**.

Another change in use of LSD reflects the different reasons why people now take the drug. Thirty years ago people took LSD as a way of unlocking eternal mysteries, and larger doses seemed to provide the key. Nowadays, a typical tab contains about 50 micrograms of the drug – about one-fifth of the 1960s dosage. This smaller amount provides a lesser experience, more in keeping with people's aim to dance or just have fun.

Other choices

For many young people, taking ecstasy is often an introduction to trying LSD. The LSD experience leads some of them to try alternative **hallucinogenic** drugs, either because they are more 'natural' or simply because they provide a different experience. These alternatives to LSD range from its powerful chemical cousin, DMT, to Cloud 9, which is the supposedly safe, all-natural version of ecstasy. Various types of mushroom, especially the psilocybe or 'magic mushroom', produce effects that are similar to those of LSD but last only about four hours.

Is LSD addictive?

Several medical texts define addiction as 'the repetitive, compulsive use of a substance, that occurs despite negative consequences to the user'. This definition is fine-tuned to distinguish between two types of **dependence** – physical and **psychological**. Heroin and alcohol are good examples of drugs that produce a physical dependence – in each case the dependent user has an overpowering compulsion to get hold of the drug, sometimes just to feel 'normal' again. On this basis, LSD cannot be said to lead to physical dependence.

All in the mind

Psychological dependence is an altogether different and more complicated issue than physical dependence. Here again, LSD is different from alcohol, for example, where a dependent drinker uses alcohol as a crutch to deal with all sorts of social occasions. The LSD user doesn't need the drug in quite the same way. Assuming that there have been no bad experiences with the drug, the LSD user will often feel a sense of sadness when coming down from the trip.

This sadness, which seems to be linked with returning to the ordinary, routine world, would be lessened by taking LSD again – or so the person thinks.

Taking LSD for several days in a row – either to avoid the sense of sadness and loss or simply for a kick – leads to a definite **tolerance** to the drug. Even on the second day an LSD user will need to take a much higher dose to achieve the same level of 'trip' as on the first day. By about the fourth day – even with constantly higher doses – the user will have no 'trip' at all. Tolerance is often considered part of the overall picture of addiction and dependence.

A regular user of LSD often adopts a new lifestyle that rejects the norms of our 'consumer society'. They may scorn 'normal' routines such as regular work or studies.

Echoes of terror

Many LSD supporters argue that the terrors of a bad trip end with the 'comedown', but this is not so. The **psychological** effects of a bad trip can linger for some time afterwards. Many people have reported feelings of depression, loss of confidence, instability and **paranoia**. The effects are magnified for those who are already vulnerable, for example people with **schizophrenia** or other mental-health conditions. Some psychologists believe that LSD might hasten – if not exactly cause – the development of schizophrenia in some people.

❝Bad setting and feeling like s*** the next day turned me off. My body freaks when I taste blotter. It says, 'Oh no, not again'.❞

Flashbacks

One of the most puzzling aspects about LSD is the experience of **flashbacks**, which can occur occasionally for several years after someone last took LSD. Some of the **hallucinogenic** elements of the last LSD trip unexpectedly reappear in a flashback, lasting only a few minutes. Some users view these simply as 'free trips' but many others are alarmed by the rapid distortion of what they see around them. Some studies indicate that up to 77 per cent of LSD users have flashbacks; others put the figure much lower, at about 15 per cent.

Although flashbacks are unpredictable, they seem to be triggered most often by anxiety, fatigue, moving about in darkness or smoking cannabis. Because flashbacks are, in effect, echoes of the last LSD experience, they can sometimes resemble a bad trip. Also, whereas someone who has a bad trip while deliberately taking LSD can usually call on friends for support, they are often left stranded during a disturbing flashback.

❝I have previously taken LSD on four occasions. The first occasion I had a 'bad trip' and on the third and fourth occasions I got flashbacks from the previous trip, experiencing the same effects.❞

(Anonymous respondents to an Ohio State University survey about LSD use)

Legal matters

LSD was first subject to special controls in the UK in 1966 when it was added to the list of drugs covered by the 1964 Drugs (Prevention of Misuse) Act. The UK position was further refined in 1971, when it was classified as a Class A drug under the Misuse of Drugs Act. This is the most serious British classification, which also includes heroin, cocaine and opium. It is illegal to possess, supply, manufacture or import LSD or even the raw ingredients (see panel) that go into its production.

Police officers display LSD ingredients found hidden in a packet of dog food.

L S D ICRODOTS
RECOVERED FROM

Arrest and conviction

In the UK, when someone is caught breaking the law, the Crime and Disorder Act requires the police to take one of the following actions. They must either issue a Reprimand or a Warning to 10-17 year olds, or if the person is over 17 they can issue an Adult Caution. The cautions can stay on police records and affect the way future offences are dealt with, for between five and eight years, or the police can decide to charge the person with an offence.

The sentence served by someone convicted of possessing or supplying LSD depends on the person's age. Up to the age of 17, people are tried in a young offenders' court, which can give a maximum sentence of one year in a young offenders' institution. People who are 18 or older go through the magistrates' courts which can impose longer sentences, although until someone is 21 they still serve their time in a young offenders' institution. The maximum sentence for an adult convicted of possession or supply is seven years' imprisonment.

In Australia, federal and state laws provide penalties which differ depending on the type of offence, the amount of the drug involved, any prior drug convictions and the law in that specific state or territory. For example, in Victoria, penalties range from fines $3000 and up to three years imprisonment to fines of $250,00 and up to 25 years imprisonment. It is also illegal to drive while under the influence of any drug.

Raw ingredients

LSD is commonly produced from lysergic acid, which itself is made from ergotamine tartrate, a substance found on an ergot fungus on rye grain. These raw ingredients are controlled by anti-drugs laws in most countries. In the United States, for example, lysergic acid and lysergic acid amide come under the Controlled Substances Act; ergotamine tartrate is regulated under the Chemical Diversion and Trafficking Act. The UK includes lysergic acid amide in its list of Class A drugs.

Life with LSD

The experience of taking LSD can be divided into two stages – the actual trip and the longer-term changes to someone's personality after taking the drug. The general affects of a trip have been discussed earlier in this book, but it is worth remembering that the trip is both vivid and disorientating. Although, strictly speaking, a person tripping on LSD will not see anything that isn't really there, the drug has enormous potential to change the senses and emotions. The changes come rapidly and unexpectedly, often leaving the user in a state of panicky and disorientated confusion.

Carrying on

Some people seem psychologically equipped to use LSD occasionally, knowing that the next trip might produce unsettling images but not being very worried about it. Although the drug produces no physical **dependence**, such a user might become attracted to the same set of circumstances that led to the first trip. This could mean entering more fully into the 'rave scene' or seeking out other venues where LSD is likely to be being used.

The negative side-effects, however, are also related to the power of the drug. A single bad trip is often enough to turn someone off LSD, and the possibility of **flashbacks** would only serve to reinforce this decision. A distinct minority of people, however, have thrown themselves wholly into the world of **psychedelic** experiences. As well as using LSD regularly – more than several times a week – they experiment with a wide range of other **hallucinatory** drugs. It is among these users, whether or not they have a history of previous mental illness, that 'acid casualties' are found. These people seem to live on the plane of altered reality that the LSD experience produces, regardless of whether they have taken the drug. They find it hard to concentrate, to study or to hold down a job that involves attention to detail. Although such abusers represent a small minority of all LSD users, their fuzzy grip on reality seems to be proof of the mysterious potential of the drug to cause harm.

Calling it quits

It need not take a bad trip or a series of disconcerting **flashbacks** to persuade someone to stop taking LSD. Some people, even if they have enjoyed their experiences with the drug, recognize the fact that ultimately the 'truths' they discover are based on chemical reactions in the brain. Whether or not they feel they have appreciated some new insights into the overall meaning of life, they feel that enough is enough.

❝I might never use it again or not for a long time if ever. The reason is that I am a nervous person to begin with and it was aggravated. I wish I could enjoy LSD and I understand its potential but I think I have to deal with my own psychological problems before I can even think about trying it again.❞

(Anonymous respondent to the Ohio State University survey on LSD use)

"In almost the same breath you will feel elated, scared, wonderful, ridiculous – part of the universal hoax, and then all these swirling certainties and uncertainties will break into fragments and begin and end again."

(Anonymous respondent to the Ohio State University survey on LSD use, describing the experience of a trip)

Treatment and counselling

LSD is a special case when compared with many other drugs of abuse. It does not produce a damaging **dependence** (as is the case with amphetamines or cocaine), it is rarely linked to violence (as with alcohol) and it does not encourage the user to resort to crime to pay for the drug (as with heroin). The picture, however, is by no means rosy. LSD produces terrifying effects in both the short and long term and it has been linked to permanent **psychological** damage.

Natural controls

Although LSD produces more dramatic psychological effects than nearly any other drug, there are certain factors that seem to act as brakes against a damaging decline in mental or physical health. Drug workers refer to the factors that keep the use of LSD in check as **governors**. LSD produces a high level of **tolerance** after only several uses in quick succession; the user will find no benefit in taking the drug too often. This tolerance cannot be overcome by taking larger doses.

Two other factors act as governors to prevent frequent abuse of LSD. The first is the length of the experience itself. With trips lasting up to twelve hours, the user is unlikely to need to buy the drug very frequently. This comparatively rare use contrasts with amphetamines and – especially – crack, drugs that abusers need to buy repeatedly and frequently to regain the feeling of a high. Finally, the unpredictable nature of an LSD trip limits the amount of times that people take the drug. After even a pleasant LSD experience, the user feels disorientated and needs time to settle. A 'bad trip' can often be enough to persuade a user to take the drug less often – if at all.

Treatment and counselling

Restoring calm

It is important to know what to do if someone is suffering the effects of a bad trip. Drug workers call the fearful effects of a bad trip 'acute panic reactions'. Reassurance is vital, along with calm persuasion that things will work out. The first thing to do is to reassure the person that they are not going to die or go mad, and that what they are feeling is the result of the drug.

It is important to take the person somewhere quiet and not to leave them alone. If qualified medical help is not available, then one or two friends should remain close by to keep the person calm. Using any type of restraint will only reinforce the person's sense of panic. In acute cases, medical personnel will sometimes provide valium or another **sedative**. Also, if they learn of any previous history of mental ill health, they will insist on making a thorough examination before releasing the person.

The Glastonbury approach

Each year the Glastonbury Festival in Somerset, England, attracts more than 100,000 young people for four days of music, dance, theatre and other spectacles. And although Michael Eavis, the owner of the farm on which it is held, points out that 'you don't need the buzz of adrenalin or any drug here,' the Festival organizers take great care to provide facilities for those who have had unpleasant drug experiences, including bad trips. Knowing that calm reassurance is as important as qualified medical care, Eavis stresses, 'We have a psychiatrist on site and a large team of welfare services to comfort, support and care for disturbed young people.'

❝I found a counsellor who talked to me about the problems with my family and other things, and gradually the flashbacks wore off. They were so frightening, sometimes they'd last for six or eight hours. The thought of drugs or alcohol really scares me now.❞

(Tanya, aged 16, discussing the lasting effects of a bad trip, in *Drugs Wise*, by Melanie McFadyean)

People to talk to

LSD has been a source of wonder and confusion, exhilaration and fear for more than fifty years. Along the way it has acquired a great deal of 'baggage' – claims that it will change the world into a better place overnight, or that it will send any first-time user on a path towards instant insanity. At the heart of all this misleading information is a core of medical knowledge, as well as sensible first-hand accounts by those who are familiar with the drug.

Friendly advice

Parents, teachers and youth workers are, in theory, the first people who should be able to provide information about LSD. Many young people are afraid to approach these groups, but it is worth stressing that drug awareness organizations are there to provide information about drugs as well as to offer help to those who have drug problems. With LSD, one of the biggest problems is getting this information, and having it provided in a confidential setting.

The UK has a wide range of telephone contacts – many of them free of charge and most of them anonymous – where young people can find out more about how alcohol and drugs are affecting them.

Many of the organizations listed in the Information and advice section (pages 52–53) are specialist phone lines. They provide the sort of telephone service described, or they can suggest local agencies throughout the UK. Some are geared specifically to queries coming from younger people.

Whether you approach one of these organizations or a family member, a youth leader or teacher, the important thing is to be able to talk – and listen – freely about LSD and the consequences of using it.

Practical details

Helplines and drugs organizations can offer practical advice on a number of aspects of LSD that are rarely mentioned. For example, the drug is a fragile chemical which can easily turn to lysergic salt when it is warmed. Lysergic salt can cause acute stomach cramps. Being able to identify such pains – and knowing that they will stop on their own – can be helpful if you are dealing with someone who is terrified by these effects. Helpline volunteers are also well placed to give details of some of the effects that result from mixing LSD with other drugs, and this knowledge can also be very helpful if someone is struggling through a bad trip.

Information and advice

The UK, like the United States, Australia and many other countries, is well served by organizations providing advice, counselling and information relating to drug use. All the contacts listed on these pages are helpful springboards for obtaining such advice or for providing confidential information over the telephone or by post.

Drug awareness contacts

ADFAM NATIONAL: Tel: 020 7928 8900
This is a national (UK) hotline for the friends and families of drug users. It provides confidential support and information to anyone who is worried about someone close to them who is using drugs.

British Association for Counselling (BAC)
1 Regent Place, Rugby CV21 2PJ
www.bac.co.uk
The BAC has an extensive directory of counselling services relating to drugs and other issues throughout the UK. Enquiries are by post only. Enclose an SAE for a list of counsellors in your area.

ISDD (Institute for the Study of Drug Dependence), Waterbridge House, 32–36 Loman Street, London SE1 OEE, Tel: 020 7928 1211, www.isdd.co.uk
The ISDD has the largest drugs reference library in Europe and provides leaflets and other publications. SCODA (Standing Committee On Drug Abuse) is located at the same address (tel: 020 7928 9500) and is one of the best UK contacts for information on drugs.

National Drugs Helpline:
Tel: 0800 776600
The helpline provides a free telephone contact for all aspects of drug use and has a database covering all of the British Isles for further information about specific drugs or regional information.

Release: Tel: 020 7603 8654
www.release.org.uk
Release operates a 24-hour helpline which provides advice on drug use and legal issues surrounding the subject.

Youth Access
1A Taylors Yard, 67 Alderbrook Road, London SW12 8AD, Tel: 020 8772 9900
Youth Access is an organization which refers young people to their local counselling service. It has a database of approximately 350 such services throughout the UK.

Contacts in the United States

Child Welfare League of America
440 First Street NW, Washington, DC 20001, Tel: 202/638-2952
www.cwla.org
The Child Welfare League of America, based in Washington, provides useful contacts across the country in most areas relating to young people's problems, many of them related to drug involvement.

DARE America
PO Box 775, Dumfries, VA 22026
Tel: 703/860-3273
www.dare-america.com
Drug Abuse Resistance and Education (DARE)
America is a national organization that links law-
enforcement and educational resources to provide
up-to-date and comprehensive information about
all aspects of drug use.

Youth Power
300 Lakeside Drive, Oakland, CA
94612, Tel: 510/451-6666, ext. 24
Youth Power is a nationwide organization
involved in widening awareness of drug-related
problems. It sponsors clubs and local affiliates
across the country in an effort to help young
people make their own sensible choices about
drugs, and to work against the negative effects
of peer pressure.

Contacts in Australia

ADCA, PO Box 269, Woden, ACT 2606
www.adca.org.au
The Alcohol and other Drug Council of Australia
(ADCA), based in the Capital Territory, gives an
overview of drug awareness organizations in
Australia. Most of their work is carried out over
the Internet but the postal address provides a
useful link for those who are not 'on-line'.

Australian Drug Foundation
409 King Street, West Melbourne
VIC 3003, Tel: 03 9278 8100
www.adf.org.au
The Australian Drug Foundation (ADF) has a wide
range of information on all aspects of drugs, their
effects and the legal position in Australia. It also
provides handy links to state- and local-based
drug organizations.

**Centre for Education and Information on
Drugs and Alcohol**
Private Mail Bag 6, Rozelle, NSW 2039
Tel: 02 9818 0401, www.ceida.net.au
The Centre for Education and Information on
Drugs and Alcohol is the ideal contact for
information on drug programmes throughout
Australia. It also has one of the most extensive
libraries on drug-related subjects in the world.

Further reading

Buzzed, by Cynthia Kuhn, Scott Swartzwelder
and Wilkie Wilson; New York and London: W.W.
Norton and Company, 1998

Drugs, by Anita Naik, part of Wise Guides
Series; London: Hodder Children's Books, 1997

Drugs: The Facts, HEA leaflet; London: Health
Education Authority, 1997

Drugs Wise, by Melanie McFadyean;
Cambridge: Icon books, 1997

*Storming Heaven: LSD and
the American Dream,* by Jay Stevens;
London: Paladin, 1989

Street Drugs, by Andrew Tyler; London:
Coronet, 3rd edition, 1995

*Taking Drugs Seriously, A Parent's Guide
to Young People's Drug Use,*
by Julian Cohen and James Kay; London:
Thorsons, 1994

The Score: Facts about Drugs, HEA
leaflet; London: Health Education Authority, 1998

Glossary

alcoholism
a disease linked to a dependence on alcohol

asylum
a place offering safety from arrest

brainwashing
using psychological methods, including drugs, to alter someone's memory

chromosomes
the elements in human cells that pass on inherited characteristics

compound
a chemical mixture

consciousness
the state of being awake and aware of one's surroundings

contradiction
a statement that is inconsistent with itself or with other statements

demoralizing
causing someone or another group to lose confidence

dependence
the physical or psychological craving for something

dilate
to widen

elite
a minority group of people who have a certain advantage, such as wealth or intelligence

enlightenment
gaining in understanding, the solution to difficult problems

flashback
an element of an LSD trip that recurs, sometimes long after the effects of the drug have worn off

governor
a factor that acts to control behaviour

hallucinations
images that people think they see, but which are not really there

hallucinogen
a substance that produces hallucinations

hallucinogenic
able to produce hallucinations

inflation
in the economy, the tendency for prices to rise so that the same amount of money has less value as time goes by

intelligence
the branch of government that deals with gathering information and spying

kaleidoscopic
having a bewildering array of moving bright colours

logo
a design or emblem that is linked to a product

market
to advertise and distribute a product widely

migraine
a severe headache, often associated with disturbed vision, that lasts for a long time

moderation
the state of not being excessive

molecule
a tiny collection of atoms

motivation
the urge to work harder or to improve oneself

mystical
having a mysterious or 'spiritual' nature

paranoia
the belief that everyone is against you

parasitic
living off another creature or plant

peer pressure
the pressure from friends of the same age
to behave in a certain way

pharmaceutical
the medical use of chemical knowledge

potent
having a powerful effect

psychedelic
relating generally to hallucinations, or
specifically to the LSD experience

psychological
to do with the mind and behaviour

recreationally
with no medical reason, for fun

respiratory
to do with the lungs and breathing

schizophrenia
a psychological condition linked to mental
confusion, causing withdrawal from society, and
sometimes associated with hearing voices in
one's mind

sedative
something to reduce tension or worry

stigma
something bad attached to a reputation, stain
on a person's character

stimulant
something to excite the body or the mind

subjective
as experienced by an individual rather than
expressed generally

suppressed
kept out of the immediate memory

synthetic
produced by humans, often in a laboratory
or factory

tolerance
the way which the body learns to expect more
of a substance

topical
to do with current events

underground
away from view, especially from the police or
other law-enforcement agencies

Index

Titles in the *Need to Know* series include:

Need to Know
Alcohol
Sean Connolly

Hardback   0 431 09779 8

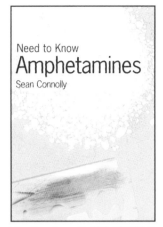

Need to Know
Amphetamines
Sean Connolly

Hardback   0 431 09777 1

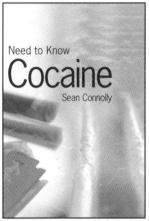

Need to Know
Cocaine
Sean Connolly

Hardback   0 431 09775 5

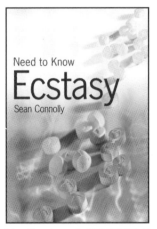

Need to Know
Ecstasy
Sean Connolly

Hardback   0 431 09781 X

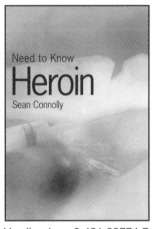

Need to Know
Heroin
Sean Connolly

Hardback   0 431 09774 7

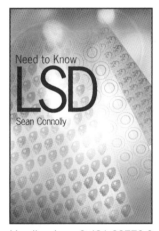

Need to Know
LSD
Sean Connolly

Hardback   0 431 09776 3

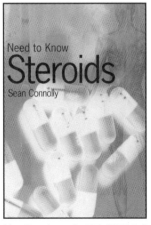

Need to Know
Steroids
Sean Connolly

Hardback   0 431 09782 8

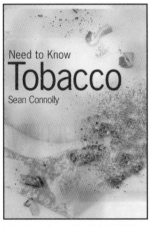

Need to Know
Tobacco
Sean Connolly

Hardback   0 431 09780 1

Find out about the other titles in this series on our website www.heinemann.co.uk/library